Geraldine & Harold Woods

THE RIGHT TO BEAR ARMS

Richard B. Morris, Consulting Editor

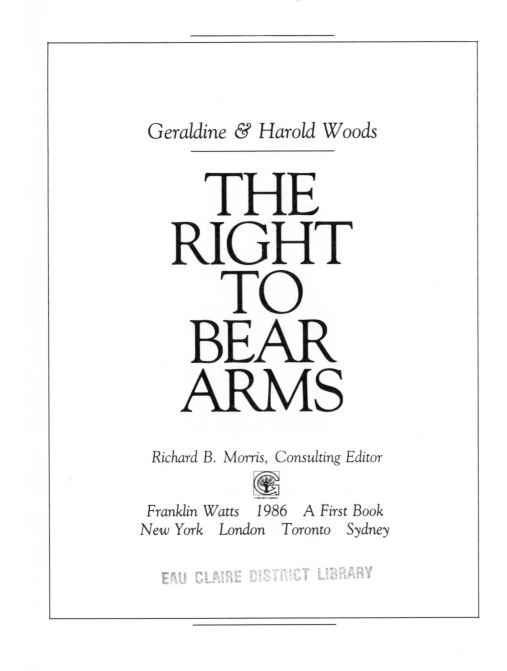

Franklin Watts   1986   A First Book
New York   London   Toronto   Sydney

Photographs courtesy of:
AP/Wide World: pp. 2, 33, 36,
39, 44, 49, 52, 55, 62; Culver Pictures, Inc.: p. 11;
Washington Area Convention and Visitors Bureau: p. 22 (top);
R. Degast/Magnum Photos, Inc.: p. 22 (bottom).

Library of Congress Cataloging-in-Publication Data

Woods, Geraldine.
The right to bear arms.

(A First book)
Bibliography: p.
Includes index.
Summary: Considers opposing interpretations of the
Constitution's Second Amendment and the right to bear
arms and presents arguments for and against gun
control. Also discusses the history of violent crime
in the United States.
1. Firearms—Law and legislation—United States—
Juvenile literature.   [1. Firearms—Law and
legislation]   I. Woods, Harold. II. Title.
KF3941.Z9W66   1986   344.73'0533   85-29500
ISBN 0-531-10109-6   347.304533

Contents

The Right to Bear Arms

Introduction

In 1981, shortly before he picked up a small pistol and a handful of bullets and went out to shoot the president of the United States, John W. Hinckley, Jr., wrote:

> See that living legend over there?
> With one little squeeze of the trigger
> I can put that person at my feet, moaning and groaning and
>   pleading with God.
> This gun gives me . . . power.
> If I wish, the President will fall and the world will look at me
>   in disbelief
> All because I own an inexpensive gun.

And this is what Ronald Reagan said, two years after he was wounded by Hinckley's bullet, in a speech to an association of gun owners:

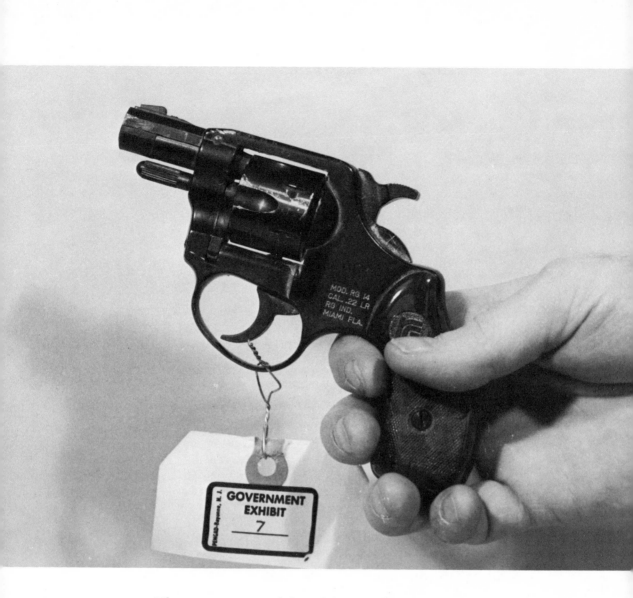

This gun was one of the exhibits used in the court case against John Hinckley, Jr., who attempted to assassinate President Ronald Reagan in March 1981.

It does my spirit good to be with people who never lose faith in America, who never stop believing in her future, and who never back down one inch from defending the constitutional freedoms that are every American's birthright.

The birthright that President Reagan was referring to is the right to bear arms. That phrase occurs in the Second Amendment to the United States Constitution. In the 200 years since the Constitution was written, the right to bear arms has often been at the center of a national debate.

Some people, like Mr. Reagan, believe that this right is a precious freedom, as important as freedom of speech, freedom of religion, and other traditional American liberties. As Mr. Reagan said, "We will never disarm any American who seeks to protect his or her family from fear and harm."

Others believe that allowing citizens to own as many weapons as they wish encourages the "one little squeeze of the trigger" that occurs far too many times a day in America. Or, as *The Straits Times* of Singapore put it after President Reagan was wounded, "The United States has preserved for its people the liberty to kill almost at will."

To understand the debate about the right to bear arms, it is necessary to go back in time, to the earliest colonial days and even before that. We must begin in England, America's mother country.

Chapter

1

*The Right to Bear Arms:
The English Tradition*

When they left the measured fields and comfortable towns of Europe for the wilderness of the New World, ordinary people took on an exciting new role: They became pioneers! However, not everything from "the old country" was left behind. European traditions and attitudes traveled to America along with the new settlers. Since most of the people in the thirteen original American colonies were English, that country's ideas on the right to keep and bear arms eventually became the basis for the Second Amendment to the United States Constitution.

Citizen Police and Soldiers

For many centuries, English towns were surrounded by high walls. At sundown the gates were closed. The men of the village kept watch in turn, guarding the sleeping townspeople within. If robbery, murder, or other crimes occurred, citizens were supposed to raise an alarm—a "hue and cry." Then the sheriff would direct all able-bodied men aged sixteen to sixty to chase the criminal.

In large cities, organized groups of volunteers helped to keep order. One of these, the London Military Foot Association, patrolled London in the eighteenth century. These duties were necessary because the first English police force was not formed until the late nineteenth century. So the ordinary Englishman was often called upon to fulfill this role.

Until the late seventeenth century, when the first permanent, or "standing," army was formed, English civilians could also be pressed into military service. These citizen-soldiers were gathered into groups called militias. They were usually commanded by the wealthy landowners or nobles of the area. Citizen militias were alerted during riots, wars, rebellions, and foreign invasions.

To be ready for these emergencies, as well as to hunt and protect their own homes, English citizens were expected to keep a variety of arms. On reporting for police or military service, each citizen brought his own weapons. The government might provide extra ammunition or arms, but in general the responsibility rested with each individual.

Some English rulers actually ordered their subjects to keep and bear arms. For example, during the reign of Alfred the Great in the ninth century, the law specified that able-bodied male citizens were to arm themselves at their own expense. In 1511, King Henry VIII commanded his subjects to possess and train with longbows. Henry's daughter Mary Tudor required civilian militias to carry their own firearms.

"To the terror of the populace"

However, the tradition of keeping and bearing arms was not unlimited. English citizens were accustomed to a variety of restrictions on the possession and use of weapons. In 1328, the Statute [law] of Northampton stated that "no man great nor small [shall] . . . go nor ride armed by Night nor by Day, in Fairs, Market, nor in the Presence of the Justices or other ministers." It also specified that Englishmen could not "go armed to the terror of the populace." In other words, unless on military or police duty, Englishmen were not to carry their weapons in public places or to use them to frighten others.

In 1383, Richard II ordered his subjects not to ride armed at all. Two hundred years later, Henry VIII banned crossbows and handguns (weapons which were often used by highwaymen) for everyone who earned less than 100 pounds a year. Since that was a large sum of money, only the richest Englishmen could use these weapons. However, almost anyone was allowed to have a gun that was over a yard (about 1 m) long, since large firearms could not easily be hidden for criminal purposes. Catholics, whom Henry considered his enemies, were prohibited almost all weapons.

Tyranny

Many of these early arms laws were probably written to protect people from robbery and murder. At times, laws restricting weapons were made in order to protect the power of the king or queen. When civil war or rebellion seemed likely, the rulers often tried to disarm their subjects, sometimes pretending that the laws were made for another purpose.

This was especially true in the seventeenth century, a time of great unrest in England. King Charles I was beheaded in 1649 after a bloody civil war, and the nonroyal government which followed was overthrown only ten years later. When Charles II came to power in 1660, he was determined to avoid his father's fate. He gathered as much power for himself as he possibly could, eliminating many of the traditional rights and privileges of the ordinary English citizen in the process.

Charles II also dealt harshly with those who opposed him. In 1662 he signed the Militia Act, which placed the crown in control of all the small civilian militias, and disbanded some which seemed likely to revolt. According to the terms of the Militia Act, the king's deputies could also search homes "dangerous to the peace of the Kingdom" and seize all weapons found there. In 1671 Charles promoted the Game Act, which reserved most weapons for those who earned more than a hundred pounds a year. The Game Act was supposed to preserve "game" animals so that only the rich could enjoy the privilege of hunting. However, it was actually an excuse to seize the weapons and ammunition of possible opponents.

Charles's laws also forbade servants to carry swords and other arms, and required gunsmiths to report the week's sales of guns and ammunition every Saturday night. No firearms could be imported from other countries, or transported within England without a license. Charles's successor, James II, passed more laws to disarm his subjects.

James II also created a permanent army. This gave the king more power because he had a group of armed soldiers to enforce his wishes—soldiers loyal only to the crown. Since the traditional civilian militias were now controlled by the king and were largely disarmed by various gun laws, people who opposed the king's policies had a hard time resisting them. To many English citizens, the standing army became a symbol of tyranny.

The English Bill of Rights

Because of these and other actions, neither king was popular. In 1688, James II was forced to flee to France. William of Orange and his wife, Mary, were invited to become England's king and queen.

A condition of the offer, however, was that the rulers agree to a declaration of rights that could not be denied to English subjects.

The declaration, which became known as the English Bill of Rights, was signed in 1689. It limited the power of the king by strengthening Parliament, the English law-making body. The bill also forbade the ruler to keep a permanent army without the consent of Parliament, and stated "That the Subjects, which are Protestants may have Arms for their Defence suitable to their Conditions, and as allowed by Law."

In later years the English citizen's right to keep and bear arms was often emphasized. Sir William Blackstone, a famous English writer on politics and law, said in 1765 that one "of the absolute rights of individuals . . . is that of having arms for their defence." Blackstone, drawing on England's experience with James II, argued that only an armed citizenry could really be free. In Blackstone's view, civilian militias checked the ruler's power and protected the people from tyranny.

This was also the view of Andrew Fletcher, an English political writer of the early eighteenth century. Fletcher stated that a good militia is "the chief part of the constitution of any free government." Another comment on the right to bear arms was made in 1780 by the recorder, an official of London. He said that "the right of his majesty's Protestant subjects to have arms for their own defence, and to use them for lawful purposes, is most clear and undeniable." However, the recorder also noted that there were limits on the legal use of arms and these limits changed according to circumstances.

By the time Blackstone, Fletcher, and the recorder of London commented on the right to bear arms, their fellow citizens had already borne them—all the way across the Atlantic! These weapons were to assist in the birth of a new nation, where the right to bear arms would become a basic liberty.

Chapter

2

A New Nation,
a New Bill of Rights

English settlers traveling to the New World carried with them the same rights guaranteed in England, including the right to bear arms. The settlers exercised that right to the fullest; firearms were everywhere in America during the colonial period. One early English visitor wrote: "There is not a Man born in America that does not understand the Use of Firearms." He added that a gun was "almost the First thing they [the colonists] Purchase and take to all the New Settlements and in the Cities you can scarcely find a Lad of 12 years That does not go a Gunning. . . ."

The early American colonists did not carry firearms for sport. Rather, they used their weapons to survive in a wild, unsettled land. Looking at the modern cities and farms of America today, it is hard to imagine the sights that met the settlers' eyes as they landed in America. There were dense forests filled with wild turkeys, deer, bears, mountain cats, and other animals. From time to time the sky would darken and seem to disappear as flocks containing millions of birds flew overhead. Every family used firearms

*These early American settlers are depicted
going to a prayer meeting.*

to hunt this wildlife for food or to defend itself against animal attacks. Many settlers also shot extra animals and traded the hides and meat for other goods. A fur trade soon sprang up between England and America and became a major source of income for some colonies.

The colonists also used guns to fight the Indians. Though many tribes had welcomed the settlers at first, some Indians later became warlike as they saw more and more of their lands claimed by European immigrants. The danger from Indian attacks in some areas was so great that men carried their guns everywhere. The colony of Georgia even passed a law in 1770 which required its citizens to bring rifles or pistols to church. Religious officials were allowed to search each man up to fourteen times a year to make sure he obeyed the law.

However, as in England, there were laws limiting the use of firearms in many colonies. In some areas, blacks and Indians were not allowed to own guns. No hunting or shooting was permitted on the streets of most towns, and using a gun to frighten other people was usually considered a crime.

Colonial Militias

In the English tradition, the colonies organized civilian militias to keep the peace. In some colonies, membership in the militia was a duty of every able-bodied male. Often, all male citizens were required to drill several days in the militia every year. Every member was expected to carry his own weapon while on duty. In New York, for example, every man was required to "provide himself, at his own Expense, with a good musket or Firelock, a sufficient Bayonet and Belt, a pouch with . . . not less than Twenty-Four Cartridges . . . two spare Flints, a Blanket and Knapsack."

*The Colonial militias were initially
organized to keep the peace.*

Most towns kept extra arms and ammunition stockpiled in case the militia members' personal guns were not adequate for a particular emergency. The militias became extremely important to the colonies as their relationship with England grew strained in the years just before the Revolutionary War.

There were many causes for the tension between England and its American colonies. One was the fact that the English government viewed the colonies as a possession of England, to be used for the benefit of the mother country. The colonies, on the other hand, believed themselves equal to any other part of England. They resented decisions from overseas which often were not to their own best advantage. Since communication with England took several months, Americans had become accustomed to making their own decisions. Throughout most of the colonial period, the royal governors who lived in each colony provided only loose supervision. So the colonists found it harder and harder to accept royal decrees as time went on.

Throughout the 1770s tension mounted, and England sent more and more soldiers to maintain its rule in America. This standing army of "Redcoats" was greatly resented, just as James II's army had been hated by English citizens 100 years earlier. In 1774, Thomas Jefferson condemned George III for sending "among us large bodies of armed forces, not made up of the people here, nor raised by the authority of our laws."

Most colonists believed that their militias could restore the liberty that the king's army took away. Samuel Stillman, a minister, wrote in 1770 that a "well-disciplined militia is . . . the security of a country." In the winter and spring of 1774 and 1775, representatives from the colonies met at assemblies and conventions to condemn the standing army and to state that "a well-regulated militia, composed of the gentlemen, freeholders, and other free-men, is the natural strength and only stable security of a free Government." Americans felt so strongly about arms that the first real battle of the Revolution took place because the English were about to seize stores of ammunition at Concord, Massachusetts.

However, even in wartime many Americans continued to support some sort of limits on weaponry. Josiah Quincy, a citizen of Boston, said that "the sword should never be in the hands of any, but those who have an interest in the safety of the community." In some towns, arms were taken away from Tories, Americans who supported union with England. At one large town assembly, members urged local governments to disarm anyone who would not join to "defend American rights."

A New Nation

On July 4, 1776, Thomas Jefferson, John Adams, Benjamin Franklin, and a number of other Americans gathered in a hot, stuffy room in Philadelphia. They had been sitting there every day for weeks listening to arguments, speeches, and votes. (Adams had written to his wife that too many of the people at the meeting loved to talk. If someone were to suggest that 2 plus 3 equaled 5, complained Adams, there would be hours of discussion before the arithmetic was accepted as correct!)

Now their work was done. As the men sat silently, they heard the secretary of their meeting read a long document that had been written by Thomas Jefferson. First, the natural rights of every person to "life, liberty, and the pursuit of happiness" were described. Then George III was condemned. The secretary proclaimed twenty-six of the king's misdeeds, including the following:

He has . . . sent . . . swarms of Officers to harass [bother] our People. . . .

He has kept among us, in times of peace, Standing Armies without the Consent of our legislature.

He has [made] the Military independent of and superior to Civilian Power.

Finally, the men heard a solemn declaration: "That these United Colonies are and of Right ought to be Free and Independent States."

Every colony accepted the Declaration of Independence. Americans no longer considered themselves part of England. They were now, in their own eyes, a free nation. However, they knew they would have to fight a bloody war before they could become independent in the eyes of England and the rest of the world.

States' Rights

Though the signers of the Declaration of Independence proclaimed freedom for the "United States," few Americans considered themselves part of a single, unified country. Nearly everyone related to his or her home state; people called themselves Rhode Islanders, Virginians, or New Yorkers. George Washington once sadly called the new country the "disunited states!"

Having just broken away from the harsh authority of George III, many Americans were also afraid of giving too much power to a central government. They did not want to substitute one tyranny for another! Many Americans believed that state governments would be easier to control and would be less likely to misuse power. So the first national government America set up after separating from England gave most of the power to individual states. In fact, the Articles of Confederation, which established the new government, stated firmly that "each State retains [keeps] its sovereignty, freedom, and independence." The Articles of Confederation entrusted the "Continental Congress"—the central United States government—with very little power.

One of the rights most states claimed for themselves after breaking away from England was the right to keep and bear arms. During the Revolution, the local militias had formed the basis of George Washington's Continental Army and had defended each state against English attacks. When the war ended, the states wanted to maintain their militias to protect themselves against possible attacks from other states, or, if necessary, from the power of the central government.

Many states condemned standing armies and affirmed the right to bear arms in declarations of rights or in their new constitutions. Virginia, for example, stated "that a well-regulated Militia, composed of the body of the people, trained to arms, is the proper, natural, and safe defence of a free State." Pennsylvania proclaimed that "the people have a right to bear arms for the defence of themselves and the state." New York's constitution contained a passage announcing "the duty of every man who enjoys the protection of society to be prepared and willing to defend it," and calling for its militia to be "at all times . . . armed and disciplined." North Carolina, Delaware, Maryland, Massachusetts, and New Hampshire also declared the right to bear arms.

As it turned out, the Continental Congress was never a danger to any state. In fact, it proved too weak to survive. It could not tax Americans, so bills mounted that could not be paid. The economy suffered because the Congress had no power to regulate trade or money. Any state could forbid trade with another, or print paper money to cover its expenses. There was no effective national court to settle arguments between states, or president to lead the government. So only a few years after the Continental Congress was created, it was replaced by a new government.

The Constitution of the United States

In May 1787, Philadelphia newspapers hailed the opening of "the Grand Convention." Fifty-five men met in the State House of Philadelphia, where the Declaration of Independence had been signed eleven years earlier. The men, representatives of each state, had come together to change the form of the United States government.

There were two main groups at the convention: the Federalists and the anti-Federalists. Federalists believed that a strong central government was necessary if the United States was to survive. Anti-Federalists, or States' Righters, were eager to preserve the freedom and power of individual states.

Throughout the long, hot summer, each side battled the other. Once, when tension was high, Ben Franklin reminded the delegates that a carpenter who was trying to fit a board into a narrow space had to cut a little wood from each side. In the same way, said Franklin, the delegates all had to be willing to give up a few of their own demands in order to make a good final product.

On September 17, 1787, the work was finished and the Constitution was signed. No delegate was completely satisfied, but only a few were completely disappointed. (One man said that he would cut off his hand before he would sign the paper, but he was in the minority!) Like Franklin's board, the Federalists and the anti-Federalists had each given up a little.

The government the convention created is the one we have today, with two houses of Congress, a president, and a Supreme Court. The federal, or central, government can tax, coin money, regulate trade, and pass laws for the entire country. The states keep many powers to balance the might of the federal government.

The Federalist Papers

Before it could take effect, the Constititution the delegates wrote had to be approved by at least nine of the thirteen states. The United States Constitution has been in existence for so long and has been so successful that it is hard to imagine how the public reacted when they first read it. Some Federalists were pleased; others thought that the central government was still too weak. Many States' Righters were dismayed; *they* thought the central government was entirely too strong! Patrick Henry, a Revolutionary War patriot and States' Righter, spoke out forcefully. "What right had they to say, 'We the People' [in the new Constitution] instead of 'We the States'?" said Henry.

Anti-Federalists were also worried about the role of state militias in the new system. According to the Constitution, the federal government could organize and equip state militias. States' Righters were afraid that the militias would then become a standing army, under the control of the federal government. Patrick Henry expressed the views of many when he said, "My great objection to this government is that it does not leave us the means of defending our rights." Another anti-Federalist, George Mason of Virginia, warned that "there should be an express declaration, that the state governments might arm and discipline [the militia]."

However, the Constitution was defended by three important

spokesmen: James Madison, Alexander Hamilton, and John Jay. These men wrote a series of eighty-five articles called *The Federalist Papers*, which explained the benefits of the new system of government. The articles were published in newspapers throughout the states and convinced many people to support the Constitution. One argued that liberty would always be assured as long as people were allowed to be "properly armed and equipped."

Noah Webster also tried to calm people's fears about the Constitution. He wrote in 1787, "Before a standing army can rule, the people must be disarmed; as they are in almost every Kingdom in Europe. The supreme power in America cannot enforce unjust laws by the sword; because the whole body of the people are armed."

The Bill of Rights

It soon became obvious that many Americans were willing to vote for the new Constitution only on the condition that it be changed, or amended, to guarantee certain rights. In fact, the constitutional conventions of Massachusetts, New York, and Virginia would not accept the document until Alexander Hamilton and others promised to add a bill of rights to it at the first possible opportunity. North Carolina and Rhode Island held out until the amendments were actually approved.

The first ten amendments, the Bill of Rights, became part of the United States Constitution on December 15, 1791. They guaranteed freedom of speech, of the press, trial by jury, and other important rights. The Second Amendment stated, "A well-regulated Militia, being necessary to the security of a free State, the right of the people to keep and bear Arms, shall not be infringed [violated]."

Chapter

3

The Second Amendment in the Courts

The Second Amendment to the Constitution seems like a simple, straightforward statement. It contains only twenty-seven words, arranged into a single sentence. Nevertheless, in the last 200 years, millions of words have been written to explain exactly what "the right to keep and bear arms" means.

There are basically two theories about the meaning of the Second Amendment. According to the militia theory, the amendment was intended to protect the right of each state to maintain an armed militia. The people who accept this theory view the right to bear arms as a collective right, held by all the citizens of a state as a group. If this interpretation is accepted, the state and federal governments may pass laws limiting the kinds of weapons individuals may own.

According to our Constitution, the federal government is responsible for equipping and organizing the state militias. (In modern times, most militias are called national guards.) This means

that the federal government buys all the weapons and may set standards and requirements for the national guards of each state. However, because of the right guaranteed in the Second Amendment, the federal government may never disarm any state's militia.

This interpretation of the Second Amendment is based on the long tradition of civilian militias in England and America. As explained earlier, citizens of both countries believed that armed militias kept the central government from becoming too powerful. People who support the militia theory feel that the Second Amendment was written only to ensure that the new American federal government did not take away the states' rights. They point out that there have always been many laws in both countries limiting the possession or use of arms by private citizens.

On the other hand, some lawyers and historians think that the Second Amendment also applies to individuals. According to this interpretation, there are actually two rights guaranteed in the amendment—the right of the states to maintain armed militias, and the right of private citizens to own and carry weapons. In this view, most laws regulating arms are not permissible because they violate an individual's "right to keep and bear arms."

People who believe in the individual-rights theory use several arguments to support their idea. Members of the English and Amer-

Top: *sometimes cases involving gun-control issues reach the U.S. Supreme Court.* Bottom: *pro- and anti-gun-control groups differ strongly in their views on gun control and the right to bear arms.*

ican militias were expected to bring their own weapons when they reported for duty. Therefore, the rights of individuals to own arms and to use them for the defense of the state may be connected. Also, the word "people" in the Second Amendment can be understood to mean "each person." The word "people" also appears in the First Amendment, which guarantees freedom of speech to individuals. The individual rights people also point to the writings of an Italian philosopher named Beccaria, who was widely read in the late eighteenth century. Thomas Jefferson copied a passage from Beccaria's works into his notebook, and John Adams quoted him in a Boston trial. Beccaria believed that arms should not be denied to innocent people just because criminals sometimes used them illegally.

The Second Amendment and the Supreme Court

The Supreme Court is the branch of government responsible for safeguarding the United States Constitution. Throughout American history, various laws passed by Congress and local governments have been challenged in the Supreme Court. The nine justices measure the law against the Constitution's principles, studying the language of the Constitution itself, earlier court decisions, and English and American tradition. If the law is declared "unconstitutional," it must be taken off the books, and anyone who was arrested for violating the law is declared innocent. If the law is judged acceptable, it is allowed to stand.

The justices also write an "opinion" for most cases, explaining the reasons for their actions. Any judge who disagrees with the majority opinion may write a separate explanation. The opinions for each case are just as important as the verdict. They are carefully studied by lawyers and judges all over the country, who apply the principles of law contained in the opinions to cases in the lower courts. Lawmakers also study Supreme Court opinions to make sure new laws do not violate the Constitution.

Though militia and individual-rights supporters continue to debate, the Supreme Court has given only one official view of the Second Amendment. The Court has ruled several times that the "right to bear arms" stated in the United States Constitution is a collective right, applying only to state militias. Time and again the Court has rejected the individual-rights point of view.

The United States
v. Cruikshank

The first Supreme Court case dealing with the Second Amendment took place in 1876. A number of white Louisiana citizens were accused of trying to prevent Levi Nelson and Alexander Tillman, two black citizens, from voting. In the opinion accompanying the case, the Court mentioned that " 'the bearing of arms for a lawful purpose' is not a right granted by The constitution." The Court also stated that the Second Amendment does nothing but "restrict the powers of the national government."

Presser v. Illinois

Ten years after the *Cruikshank* decision, a man named Herman Presser was arrested for drilling his own private army. Presser, mounted on horseback and carrying a cavalry sword, had led 400 men armed with rifles through the streets of Chicago. Presser was convicted and fined $10 for his crime. He appealed the case all the way to the Supreme Court, claiming that his right to bear arms had been violated.

The Court again ruled that the Second Amendment only protects state militias from being disarmed by the federal government. The Court also said that state and federal laws can regulate when and in what manner individuals can possess firearms.

Miller v. Texas

On July 23, 1892, a Texan named Miller was found guilty of murdering a Mr. Riddle and sentenced to death. Miller appealed the verdict, claiming that his arrest had been based partly on the fact that he was carrying a pistol. According to Texas law at that time, carrying dangerous weapons, including firearms, was illegal. Miller claimed that the law was unconstitutional because it violated his right to bear arms. Miller hoped that the case against him could be weakened enough so that his murder conviction would be overturned. Unfortunately for Mr. Miller, the Supreme Court ruled that the Texan law was constitutional, since the Second Amendment limited only the power of the federal government and had nothing to do with state laws.

United States v. Miller

In the sixteenth century, Henry VIII prohibited most of the citizens of England from carrying a firearm less than a yard (about 1 meter) long, since such weapons were often used by highwaymen. Four hundred years later, the Congress of the United States passed a similar law. "Sawed-off shotguns"—long guns with barrels shortened to less than 18 inches (about 46 centimeters)—were not to be transported across state lines unless they were registered, taxed, and stamped by government officials.

In 1939, Jack Miller and Frank Layton broke that law. They carried a "double barrel 12 gauge Stevens shotgun with a barrel less than 18 inches in length" from Claremore, Oklahoma, to Siloam Springs, Arkansas. The police officer who arrested Miller and Layton noted that the weapon was not stamped.

When the case reached the Supreme Court, the law regulating the shotgun was held to be constitutional. According to the opinion, the possession of such a weapon had no "reasonable relation to the preservation or efficiency of a well-regulated militia, and therefore [the Court] cannot say that the second amendment guarantees to the citizen the right to keep and bear such a weapon."

Quilici v. the Village of Norton Grove

On June 8, 1981, the village of Morton Grove, Illinois, passed ordinance [law] number 81-11. Ordinarily, Morton Grove's ordinances are of interest only to the town's 24,000 residents. New laws may be reported in the *Morton Grove Life and Champion*, the local paper, but usually they attract little attention anywhere else.

Ordinance 81-11 was different, however. Soon after its passage, newspapers, magazines, and television stations all across the country made it a headline story. Fierce debate broke out. Morton Grove was called everything from "Moron Grove" to the most courageous town in America.

All of this resulted from ordinance 81-11, which made Morton Grove the first town in the United States to ban the possession of handguns by all private citizens, except for police, military personnel, and prison officials, and licensed gun collectors or gun clubs. Citizens who owned handguns were required to bring them to the police station or risk breaking the law.

Members of the National Rifle Association, a group that favors the legal use of firearms, went to court to argue that Morton Grove's ordinance violated their constitutional rights. The National Rifle Association based its case on the section of the Illinois state constitution which says, "Subject only to police power, the right of the individual citizen to keep and bear arms shall not be infringed [violated]."

When the case reached the United States Supreme Court in 1983, the justices, without comment, refused to hear it. Therefore, the judgment of the lower court still stands. This was a defeat for the National Rifle Association, since the lower court had ruled that the "possession of handguns by individuals is not part of the right to keep and bear arms." The lower court also explained that local and state governments have the right to pass laws protecting public health and safety, including a ban on handguns.

*Can the Court
Change Its Mind?*

The National Rifle Association has now begun a new case in the Illinois state courts and still hopes to overturn Morton Grove's ordinance 81-11. It is obvious that people who support the individual rights interpretation have not given up, in spite of all the court decisions against them. This may be because the Supreme Court does change from time to time, as society itself changes. When justices retire, their replacements may have different beliefs or different ways of looking at the law.

Two civil rights cases are a good example of this. In a case known as *Plessy* v. *Ferguson*, the Court ruled in 1896 that separate schools for black and white students were permissible, as long as both provided the same quality of education. Half a century later, however, this "separate but equal" ruling was overthrown. In *Brown* v. *the Board of Education* (1954), the Court decided that separate schools for different races could never really be equal. All-black or all-white schools were therefore illegal, since people of every race are entitled to equal treatment according to United States law.

Other Court Decisions

Not every case involving the right to bear arms has gone all the way to the Supreme Court. There have been many state rulings on gun control laws that were never brought before the nation's highest court. Many of these were based on state constitutional guarantees of the right to bear arms, which are given by thirty-eight of the fifty American states.

Some of the lower-court decisions have supported the "militia" view of the amendment, and others have favored the "individual rights" interpretation. Important cases include:

Salina v. *Blaksley*. This was a 1905 Kansas case in which the "militia" view was strongly upheld.

Superior Court of Michigan (1931). The court supported a ban on individual possession of blackjacks, bombs, and rockets, saying that "some arms . . . are too dangerous to be kept in a settled community by an individual . . . and have legitimate employment only by guards and police."

Schubert v. *DeBard*. In this 1980 case the Supreme Court of Indiana ruled that citizens do not have to show that they need a gun in order to obtain a license for one. This case supports the "individual rights" view.

Oregon State v. *Kessler.* In 1980, police arrested a man for possessing two billy clubs. The man was found guilty by lower courts, but the Oregon Supreme Court ruled that citizens of Oregon have a right to arms for their personal defense.

The debate continues between those who believe in the individual-rights view and those who favor the militia interpretation of the Second Amendment. The debate tends to turn into an argument whenever a new law limiting firearms is considered. In the next chapter, we will examine some of the arms control regulations in existence in the United States today.

Chapter

4

Restrictions on the
Right to Bear Arms

One reason why the right to bear arms has been examined by the U.S. Supreme Court so often is that firearms have never faded from the American scene. After the colonial days, Americans began to move across the continent. Firearms gave the settlers a great advantage during the many Indian wars. Guns were also part of many westerners' working equipment; cowboys needed their firearms to hunt, control stampedes, and shoot animals that threatened their cattle. Since the American frontier was a vast, untamed area with few law officers, most pioneers also relied on guns for defense against crime.

The First Gun Control Laws

In the 1920s and 1930s, a new type of real-life gunslinger appeared. During these decades, the public was terrified by groups of armed criminals. Al Capone, John Dillinger, Bonnie and Clyde, and other gangsters blasted their way across the country with submachine guns—weapons that could quickly fire a whole belt of bullets without stopping. Another type of firearm favored by the mobs was the sawed-off shotgun, which was powerful and easy to conceal.

During the frontier era, there were a few local laws regulating firearms, but no nationwide controls on guns. As gangster violence grew, a federal law to control firearms was passed. The Mailing of Firearms Act of 1927 prohibited anyone but police, the military, and arms dealers from sending pistols and revolvers through the United States mail. However, this law did not accomplish much since it was still legal to transport firearms by private delivery service.

Congress soon realized that stronger measures were needed. The National Firearms Act of 1934 registered and heavily taxed "gangster type" weapons: machine guns, sawed-off shotguns, and silencers. Four years later, the Federal Firearms Act of 1938 added more restrictions on guns. Manufacturers, dealers, and importers of weapons who did business in more than one state now needed federal licenses and were required to keep records of all sales. Firearms could not be mailed across state lines to anyone who was currently under arrest or who had been convicted of a serious crime.

Some people credit these laws with the fact that machine guns and other gangster weapons are seldom used in crimes today. How-

These weapons were abandoned by John Dillinger when he escaped from Federal agents at a Wisconsin resort in April 1934.

ever, both the 1934 and 1938 laws had many loopholes in them, and did little to control handguns.

The Gun Control Act of 1968

In the 1960s, there was another surge in firearms violence. During those years, the country was shocked by the assassinations of President John Kennedy, his brother Robert Kennedy, and Martin Luther King, Jr. The decade was also filled with many demonstrations. Throughout the country, black people organized to gain their civil rights, and many Americans protested the Vietnam War. While most of these demonstrations were peaceful, some turned into riots. Also, a few radical groups proclaimed violence as the only way to change things in America.

In response to these problems, Congress passed the Gun Control Act of 1968. This law, which is still in effect today, sets twenty-one as the minimum age to buy handguns and eighteen as the minimum age to buy rifles and shotguns without written consent from a parent. With few exceptions, the law allows no one to buy firearms outside of his or her home state. The Gun Control Act also requires dealers selling handguns to check the purchaser's identification and to record the purchaser's name, address, and physical description. Everyone buying a handgun also has to fill out a federal form saying that he or she has never been convicted of a serious crime, has no mental problems, and is not a fugitive or a drug addict.

The Gun Control Act also prohibits imports of small, cheap pistols called Saturday Night Specials. The name comes from the idea that the guns could be used to settle Saturday night arguments. Saturday Night Specials, also called snubbies, have barrels only 2 or 3 inches (5 to 8 centimeters) long. They have few sporting uses and are often used for crime since they are so easy to hide. According to a study conducted between 1973 and 1979 by the United States Bureau of Alcohol, Tobacco, and Firearms, 67 to 73 percent of the handguns used in crimes were Saturday Night Specials. Saturday Night Specials were used to kill former Beatle John Lennon and to wound President Reagan. By prohibiting imported Saturday Night Specials, sponsors of the Gun Control Act hoped that the level of handgun violence would drop.

The Gun Control Act of 1968 did not accomplish everything it set out to do. For one thing, manufacturers of Saturday Night Specials have continued to market their products. Instead of sending handguns to the United States, they now send handgun *parts*. These parts are assembled in America, and the finished snubbies are put on sale.

Another problem is the restriction against selling guns to criminals, mentally ill people, and drug addicts. The law requires handgun buyers to state that they do not belong to one of these groups. However, the dealer does not have to check that the purchaser's statement is true. So all the purchasers have to do is lie! There is nothing in the Gun Control Act of 1968 to insure that members of the prohibited groups do not buy guns.

State and Local Laws

The laws described above are federal laws; they apply to the entire country and cannot be weakened by any local government. In other words, no state or city can decide to allow thirteen-year-olds to purchase handguns. However, local areas do have the right to pass stricter gun regulations if they wish.

There are now over 20,000 state and city laws controlling firearms. Most concentrate on handguns. For one thing, handguns

are the weapon most often used in connection with crimes in the United States. Although only 25 to 30 percent of all the firearms in the nation are handguns, these weapons account for 75 percent of all murders committed with firearms and 95 percent of all armed robberies. This is probably because handguns are small and easily concealed. Also, handguns are not often used for hunting, as rifles and shotguns are. In a national survey of gun owners, 90 percent mentioned hunting as a good reason for owning a long gun, but only 16 percent said the same thing about handguns.

There are several types of handgun control laws:

Sales. Some states regulate dealers, requiring special licenses or restricting sales by private individuals.

Registration. In some areas, gun owners must report the serial numbers of their weapons to the police and give notice if a gun is sold. Cleveland and other cities require a handgun-owner identification card.

Licensing. Some cities, such as New York, require a license for each gun. Before a license is issued, the gun buyer must be checked by the police. People who have criminal records, mental problems, or who cannot prove that they need the gun may be denied a license. Licenses may be limited to one area; a gun owner may be allowed to keep a gun at home, for example, but not at work.

Carrying. Many states require special licenses to carry firearms either concealed or openly. Some states prohibit carrying a weapon

*Mourners at a service for
John Lennon in Chicago*

at all. A few states require licenses to transport a handgun in an automobile.

Waiting period. In some states, you can buy a handgun and leave the store with it the same day. Other states make the purchaser wait up to three weeks before allowing the sale to be completed. This waiting period may give the police time to check the gun buyer's background, or allow people who want to commit a crime time to "cool off" and reconsider their actions.

Bans. Washington, D.C., bans the purchase of new handguns, though weapons owned before 1976 may be kept. Morton Grove, Illinois, bans handguns for almost all private citizens.

Two Rights in Conflict

What do gun control laws do? Secure every American's right to live in peace? Or violate every American's right to bear arms?

People who choose the first answer, the procontrol group, usually want to keep and even strengthen the firearms laws already in effect. They feel that these laws are necessary to stop the rise in violent crime and to ensure public safety. Few people in this group believe that all guns should be banned, and even fewer people believe that all guns *could* be banned. As one writer put it, unless you held a giant magnet over the United States, there would be no way to gather all the firearms in the country into one place! However, in the opinion of procontrol Americans, handguns are dangerous weapons and should be strictly regulated.

People who choose the second answer, the anticontrol group, support fewer restrictions on firearms. In general, they believe that guns should be denied to young children, to the mentally ill, and to criminals. However, they firmly believe that every mature, law-

Guns interest adults—and children.

abiding citizen who wishes to own and carry a gun should be able to do so. They feel that any limit on the legal use of firearms is a violation of their rights to bear arms and to defend themselves and their property.

In the chapters that follow, we will examine the arguments on each side of this debate: procontrol in Chapter Five, anticontrol in Chapter Six.

Chapter

5

Arms in
America Today

Experts estimate that there are currently over 150 million firearms in the United States. A new handgun is sold in the United States *every twelve seconds*. To gun control supporters, the situation is simple. This huge arsenal of weapons is directly connected to the following facts:

The United States has one of the highest rates of violence by firearms in the world.

Over 23,000 Americans die from handgun violence every year. That's one death every fifty-two minutes.

Since 1963, guns have been responsible for the deaths of 400,000 Americans—more than the number of U.S. soldiers who died in World War II.

Handguns are the fifth leading cause of death among children in America.

Pro–gun control people have many powerful arguments to support their ideas. Let's look at each in turn.

Crime and Self-Defense

It happens a hundred times every day. Someone comes home and finds the door open, a window smashed, or the lock unlatched. Inside, there is confusion: drawers dumped out, books pulled off shelves, clothes on the floor. Something's missing—the television, a piece of jewelry, a sum of money. Usually, a homeowner's first reaction is relief that no one was in the house during the burglary. Later, many people's second reaction is to buy a gun—to be ready for the next time.

Is this a good idea? According to the FBI, 99 percent of all burglaries occur when no one is at home. So the gun will probably never be used to scare a burglar. Even if a thief does meet the victim, there may not be time to find the firearm. A National Crime Survey found that only 3.5 percent of gun owners had the opportunity to use their guns when they were robbed on the street or at home. Furthermore, experts estimate that over 500,000 handguns are stolen every year. The law-abiding householder who keeps a gun for protection will probably never use it. If the house is broken into, however, the gun may be stolen and used by a criminal in a future crime. In some areas, police estimate that 50 percent of all handgun crimes are committed with stolen weapons.

Another problem is that a loaded gun in the house can be dangerous. The FBI reports that a firearm kept in the home for self-defense is six times more likely to kill a relative or a friend than a burglar. The problem is that if a handgun is to be available for self-defense, it must be kept loaded and in an easy-to-reach place. Unfortunately, a loaded gun that is handy for the adults of the house is also handy for children, and that means danger. Each year, hundreds of children die from accidental gunshot wounds. A 1981 report from the United States surgeon general blamed handguns for an "epidemic" of deaths and injuries among children.

Adults, too, are at risk. Fifty-seven percent of all murders involve family members or friends. Many of these crimes take place on the spur of the moment, perhaps in a drunken fit or in a jealous rage. People who want stronger gun controls don't claim that just the presence of firearms in a house causes crime. However, according to some experts, America's high crime rate, both inside and outside the house, may result partly from the fact that it is so easy to kill with a handgun. Murderers, muggers, and other criminals do not even have to touch their victims, risking injury to themselves. They pull the trigger and the bullet goes out instantly—an effortless act. There's no need for criminals to even dirty their hands!

Whether or not this theory is true, statistics show that the more handguns there are in an area, the more gun-related crimes are committed. In 1979, a national committee studying juvenile delinquency came to the conclusion that easily available handguns contribute to the number of violent deaths and injuries among young people.

Pro–gun control people also point out that an attack from a gun is normally far more serious and life threatening than one from almost any other type of weapon. According to a study done in Chicago in 1975, gun attacks were almost five times more likely to result in death than knife attacks. So while gun controls may not stop crime completely, they may reduce the number of deaths and serious injuries resulting from firearms.

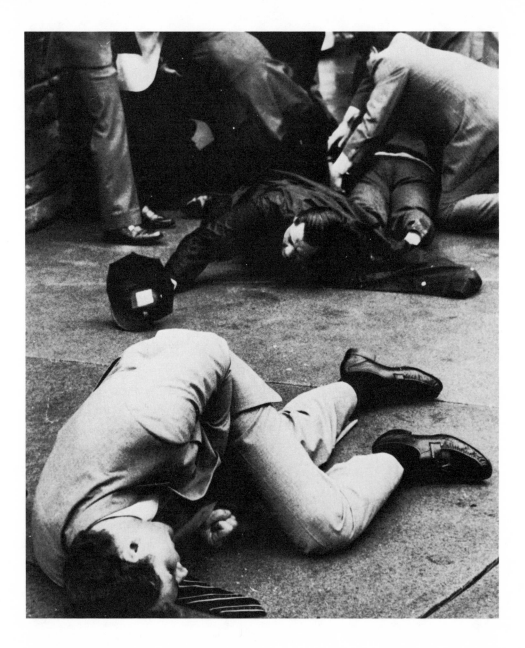

Assassinations

On October 13, 1980, a young man walked into Rocky's Pawn Shop in Dallas, Texas. He selected a six-shot, .22-caliber revolver and filled out the form required by law. No, he wrote, he was not a drug addict. No, he had never been convicted of a major crime. And no, he was not mentally ill. He paid $47.50, plus a $10 federal fee, and left with his new handgun.

A few months later the young man, whose name was John W. Hinckley, Jr., used his revolver to shoot President Ronald Reagan. Fortunately, President Reagan, as well as his press secretary, James Brady, and two others who were also injured in the attack, survived. Hinckley himself now divides his days between prison and a mental hospital. According to federal law, he will be imprisoned for the rest of his life.

President Reagan was just another in a long line of American presidents, ex-presidents, and candidates who have been shot or threatened by firearms. The list includes:

Andrew Jackson, 1835, attempt
Abraham Lincoln, 1865, killed

The scene at the attempt by John Hinckley, Jr., to assassinate President Reagan. On the ground, with his head in the foreground, is James Brady, at the time the Presidential Press Secretary.

James Garfield, 1881, killed
William McKinley, 1901, killed
Theodore Roosevelt, ex-president, 1912, wounded
Franklin Roosevelt, 1933, attempt
Harry Truman, 1950, attempt
John F. Kennedy, 1963, killed
Robert Kennedy, candidate, 1968, killed
George Wallace, candidate, 1972, wounded
Gerald Ford, 1975, two attempts
Ronald Reagan, 1981, wounded

Of course, if the list is expanded to include more than government leaders, many others, such as civil rights crusader Martin Luther King, Jr., Congressman Allard Lowenstein, and former Beatle John Lennon, could be added.

After each killing, thousands of newspaper articles are written to explain why, as one person commented, "violence is as American as apple pie." Everyone wonders what can be done to stop the bloodshed. To people who favor gun control, at least part of the answer is simple: Strictly regulate handguns, which are most used by assassins, and fewer leaders will die. This viewpoint is supported by a survey the Associated Press conducted in April 1981, which found that countries where assassinations are rare almost always have strict gun control laws.

Suicides

Each year, over 10,000 suicides result from handgun injuries. Opponents of gun control laws say that if someone wants to commit suicide, he or she will do so no matter what. If a gun is not available, they point out, many other weapons are.

However, people who recover from suicide attempts often receive treatment and go on to live normal lives. The key word here is "recover." Since most handguns can kill instantly, there are usually no second chances with a bullet.

Some studies have also shown that the number of handguns in circulation is related to the number of suicides. As the number of households with guns in them rises, so does the suicide rate. Areas with strict gun control laws and low rates of gun ownership also have lower suicide rates.

Do Gun Controls Work?

It is difficult to tell if the gun control laws already in existence actually lower the crime rate. The problem is that each state has different requirements. A criminal may buy a gun legally in one state, where there are few regulations, and use it in another, where gun controls are very strict.

This is what John Hinckley did. He bought his gun in Texas, which has very few restrictions, and fired it at President Reagan in Washington, D.C., which has one of the toughest gun control laws in the country. Since 1977, it has been illegal to carry a pistol outside the home in Washington, and all guns must be registered.

According to gun control supporters, the attack on President Reagan was not really a failure of the Washington, D.C., gun law. They point out that in the first three years after the law was passed, Washington's murder rate dropped by 25 percent. They also note that areas in the United States with the weakest handgun laws and the highest rates of gun ownership have the highest murder rates. Gun control supporters feel that strict, nationwide gun control regulations will bring a uniform decrease in crime throughout the United States.

To really see the effect of firearms regulations on crime, pro–gun control people believe that it is necessary to look at countries where strict limits have been placed on firearms. In Britain and Canada, for example, it is extremely difficult for a private citizen to purchase a handgun. In 1980, *eight* people were murdered with guns in each of those nations. In the same year, 11,522 persons were murdered with handguns in the United States. Other countries with strict handgun regulations, such as Japan, Sweden, and West Germany, also have low rates of violent crime. This is even true in Switzerland, where handguns are restricted but where every able-bodied man is required to own and know how to use a rifle.

The Experts' Opinion

Since 1967, seven national commissions, composed of experts on crime and justice, have recommended stronger controls on handguns:

> The 1981 Attorney General's Task Force on Violent Crime proposed a required background check on all handgun buyers and a ban on the import of Saturday Night Special parts.

> The 1979 National Advisory Committee for Juvenile Justice and Delinquency Prevention recommended a ban on the manufacture and sale of most handguns.

> Two commissions studying criminal law in 1971 and 1973 said that handguns should be limited to police and military officers.

Some of the guns collected when Baltimore, Maryland, residents were paid a bounty of $50 for turning in a gun

The 1969 National Commission on the Causes and Prevention of Violence concluded that national licensing, safety tests, and regulation of firearms dealers was necessary. The commission also said that a government fund should be established to purchase handguns from private citizens.

National crime commissions recommended stricter controls on firearms and ammunition in 1967 and 1968.

Another kind of expert—a criminal instead of a police official—may have the last word on the subject. From his jail cell, John W. Hinckley, Jr., President Reagan's attacker, stated that he was considering a contribution to a pro–gun control group. He said, "If somebody like me can buy six Saturday Night Specials, there is something drastically [extremely] wrong."

Chapter

6

The Case Against Gun Control

"Guns don't kill; people do." In one sentence, that's the message opponents of gun control would like to get across. For the most part, they are just as horrified by crime as anyone else. However, as they see it, a small piece of metal cannot be blamed for all the forces in society that cause crime. Poverty, lack of values, a breakdown of the justice system, troubled homes, and many other factors push people to break the law. The gun, they believe, is only a tool, not the reason crimes are committed.

Opponents of gun control also feel that a law to ban handguns, such as the one in Morton Grove, takes away the right of innocent people to bear arms because of crimes committed by others. After all, fewer than one gun owner in 3,000 ever commits murder. Millions of Americans who own firearms use them for legal purposes. Police officers, military personnel, security guards, and others often carry guns while on the job. Many Americans also enjoy hunting, the sport of target shooting, or collecting fine and antique weapons.

With soaring crime rates, more and more Americans also view guns as a necessary tool of self-defense. Advertisements printed in progun publications often show a worried police officer announcing, "I can't be everywhere," or a crime victim asking sorrowfully, "Where were the police when I was mugged?" To these citizens, guns are the great equalizers. The weapons enable young and old, male and female, strong and weak citizens alike to meet criminals on equal terms.

Progunners also feel that the study which showed that handguns are more likely to kill family or friends than criminals is misleading. The researchers compared only the deaths by firearms of criminals and people known to the gun owner. There was no mention of the number of burglars, muggers, and other attackers who were wounded or simply scared away by the presence of the gun. So progun people believe that the true usefulness of firearms for self-defense was not revealed.

If Guns Are Outlawed

People who oppose gun control often see these laws as a grave threat to their own safety. This is the theme of another anti–gun control slogan: "If guns are outlawed, only outlaws will have guns." They feel that since criminals have no respect for laws anyway, only law-abiding citizens will obey gun control regulations. Criminals will simply ignore them!

A display in a New Jersey sporting goods store

In New York City, for example, where gun control laws are among the strictest in the country, experts estimate that one to two million illegal guns are in circulation. Gun control opponents fear that such laws leave good citizens defenseless, with only understaffed and overworked police forces for protection. This view is supported by a poll of 34,000 chiefs of police, sheriffs, and police officers from across the United States. Over 80 percent felt that criminals rather than citizens would benefit most from the banning of handguns.

Violent crime has been reduced in some areas where criminals know their victims may be armed. In 1968, 6,000 women in Orlando, Florida, took a course on how to handle and fire a gun. The number of rapes in Orlando decreased by 90 percent in the following year; the rates of burglary and assault (armed attack) also dropped. In Highland Park, Michigan, there were no armed robberies for four months after merchants took a firearms course. Before the course began, Highland Park had an average of 1.5 robberies a day. After a similar course was given to grocers in Detroit, the number of armed robberies dropped by 90 percent. All these courses were widely reported in newspapers and on television and radio. Criminals may have been frightened off by the possibility of violent resistance.

Assassinations

On March 20, 1974, an assassin shot at a car carrying Princess Anne of England. Fortunately, he missed. This is only one example of firearms violence in the United Kingdom: three years earlier, a gunman had fired over thirty shots from a submachine gun at the Jordanian ambassador to Britain. In 1977, the former prime minister of Yemen was shot and killed as he sat in a car outside a

In Kennesaw, Georgia, an Atlanta suburb with a population
of 5,400 in 1982, each head of household must own and maintain
a firearm and ammunition. This picture shows a pawnshop owner
and a display of handguns on the day the law went into effect.

London hotel. In 1978, there were three attacks with firearms on Arab leaders visiting England, and one submachine gun assault on a bus carrying an Israeli flight crew to a British airport.

All these incidents are noted by gun control opponents because handguns are banned for almost all private citizens in England. Though Britain has not lost its heads of state to firearms as America has, the country has still suffered from political violence. In France, Premier Charles de Gaulle survived thirty-one assassination attempts between 1944 and 1966, despite strict controls on handguns in that country.

Progun people also point out that countries whose national leaders have been attacked in recent years have a wide range of gun control laws. In some, the death penalty may be given for simply possessing a gun. In others, there are few restrictions on firearms. All of this, according to progun people, shows that handgun control does not really solve the problem of assassination.

Accidents and Suicides

Banning guns to reduce the number of accidents, according to progun people, is simply not fair to responsible gun owners. The National Safety Council conducted a ten-year study of the causes of accidental death between 1960 and 1970. The official rankings were (1) cars, (2) falls, (3) drowning, (4) burns, (5) poison, and (6) firearms. Progun people point out that no one dreams of banning cars to reduce the number of fatal crashes.

To combat accidental gun injuries, many gun owners recommend safety courses for users and their families. In one school program, for example, young children act out various situations using a toy pistol. The teacher stops them from time to time and asks questions: "Is anyone in danger now? Could the gun go off? What should you do if you see someone handling a gun like this?"

Approaching the problem of suicide through gun control is also wrong, in the opinion of progun people. If mentally disturbed people really want to commit suicide, gun regulations will not be enough to stop them. Simply too many other methods are available: pills, falls, knives, and so forth. In a recent year, the United States had 12.2 suicide deaths for every 100,000 citizens. West Germany, Japan, France, Sweden, Denmark, and Canada all had higher suicide rates, in spite of extremely strict gun control laws.

As with accidents, most gun owners see no need to give up their rights to use firearms properly just because some people misuse guns. Many gun owners compare their weapons to alcohol. The great majority of people use alcohol sensibly, as part of their recreation. A few become alcoholics, who, without treatment, can drink themselves to death. Yet prohibition of all alcoholic beverages, which took place in the early part of this century, was a failure. Alcohol was widely available, even though it was illegal. Problem drinkers continued to get drunk, and those who had never misused alcohol were deprived of their rights.

Do Gun Controls Work?

Progun people believe they have evidence showing that gun laws don't work. Twenty percent of all murders in the United States occur in only four cities: New York, Washington, Detroit, and Chicago. Yet these cities have the toughest gun control laws in the nation. In Massachusetts, a law was passed requiring a one-year prison term for anyone possessing an unlicensed firearm. The number of murders committed with firearms decreased when the new law took effect. However, street crime rates in Massachusetts stayed high, since many criminals substituted knives and clubs for their guns. Also, according to a 1976 study done by the University of Wisconsin, strict gun control laws don't discourage criminals from committing crimes.

Opponents of gun control have also studied the results of firearms restrictions in other countries. In Taiwan, where all private ownership of handguns is banned, the murder rate is twice that of the United States. The example of Jamaica is even more extreme. No private citizen of the island is permitted to own a firearm or ammunition. Possession of even a single bullet is punishable by life in prison! Yet Jamaica has more gun deaths than Washington, D.C., one of our nation's most violent cities.

Instead of restrictions on all firearms, which would limit both law-abiding and criminal users of the weapons, many gun owners favor another approach. They recommend strict, required penalties for all crimes committed with guns. Any criminal using a gun would have to serve a year or more in prison, in addition to the regular sentence for the crime. In this way people who misuse guns will be punished, and innocent gun owners will not be affected.

This idea has been tried in eighteen states, with mixed results. Florida is a good example. Officials there found that required sentences did not lead to a lower crime rate or more time in prison for criminals. Although judges had no choice about the sentence, prosecutors often allowed criminals to plead guilty to a lesser charge with a smaller penalty. The murder rate in Florida continues to increase. In other areas, some experts believe that the required sentencing laws have discouraged criminals.

Ronald Reagan, himself a victim of handgun violence, believes that required sentences are the only just and workable form of gun control. At one press conference he said, ". . . never mind whether you're going to try to take guns away from the good people, the criminal is going to find a way to have a gun." In another speech he added, "Guns don't make criminals. Hard-core criminals use guns. And locking . . . the hardcore criminals up, and throwing away the key, is the best gun control law we could ever have."

What Does America Want?

According to a recent Gallup poll, seven out of ten Americans want tougher gun control laws. In the same poll, nine out of ten people said that they favored a waiting period between the time a gun is requested and actually sold. A 1980 Gallup poll showed that 65 percent of gun owners approve of requiring a police permit to purchase a handgun. Earlier, a 1975 Gallup poll reported that more than half of all Americans favored an outright ban on the private ownership of handguns.

However, these numbers may be misleading. When new gun laws come up for a vote, they are often defeated. In 1982, for example, Californians soundly defeated a tough new gun control law called proposition 15. Proposition 15 would have required the registration of all handguns and a freeze on the number of firearms a citizen could possess. Proposition 15 also provided for a six-month jail term for possession of an unlicensed, concealable firearm.

American voters, through their elected representatives, have also defeated several other strong gun control laws. For the past several years, Senator Edward Kennedy (whose two brothers were shot and killed) and Representative Peter Rodino have sponsored a bill in Congress to limit firearms. The Kennedy-Rodino Bill has never received the support it needs in Congress to be made into law.

The bill would:

Require an extra two to five years in jail for anyone using a handgun to commit a serious crime.

Forbid carrying a handgun without a permit.

Limit purchases of new handguns to two a year.

Ban the manufacture and sale of Saturday Night Specials in the United States.

Call for a twenty-one-day waiting period between the time a buyer selects and receives a handgun. During the twenty-one days, the police and FBI can check on the purchaser's background.

Teflon Bullets

Another bill regulating firearms may have better luck in Congress than the Kennedy-Rodino Bill. This bill concentrates on ammunition, specifically, on teflon bullets. Most people think of teflon as the nonstick coating on frying pans. However, teflon and other substances like it can also be used to coat special, superhard bullets. These bullets are called "armor piercing" because they can penetrate up to four bulletproof vests. For this reason they are especially dangerous to police officers.

The National Rifle Association is opposed to a ban on armor piercing bullets because it feels that the law would also limit ammunition used by hunters. However, supporters of the bill believe that the new law would have a very small effect on hunters and would save many lives. At this point the bill is still being considered in Congress.

Pro-Gun Bills

Another new bill, the Firearm Owners Protection Bill, was passed by the Senate in 1985. If it is approved in the House of Representatives, President Reagan has said he will sign it into law. The Firearm Owners Protection Bill was written by Senator James McClure and Representative Harold Volkmer. It takes away some of the restrictions placed on gun owners by the Gun Control Act of 1968 and other laws. The Firearm Owners Protection Bill would:

> Make it legal for someone to buy a gun outside of his or her home state, as long as certain conditions are met.

> Allow federal agents to inspect gun dealers' records only once a year. Currently, records can be inspected at any time.

> Allow firearms to be transported through any state without regard for that state's gun laws, as long as the weapon remained locked up. In other words, someone could drive through New York with a handgun locked in the trunk of a car without getting a New York State permit.

Congress is also considering several other laws that favor gun owners. One bill would allow people who legally possess firearms in their own communities to carry them anywhere in the United States, regardless of local laws. Another would protect gun owners from lawsuits if their guns are stolen and used to commit a crime. Lastly, there is a bill to prevent manufacturers of guns from being sued if the weapons they have made cause injury or death.

The last two bills were proposed because recently several victims of handgun crimes have gone to court against gun manufac-

Representative Peter Rodino, House Speaker Thomas P. O'Neill, Jr.,
and Senator Edward M. Kennedy (left to right) shown in
May 1982 with 500,000 petitions advocating handgun control.

turers and owners. The victims are seeking money for medical bills and other expenses; they claim that the people who make and own guns are responsible for the damage their weapons cause.

Two Points of View

George Washington, Alexander Hamilton, and other Founding Fathers could not have imagined such issues as teflon bullets, Saturday Night Specials, and handgun licenses when they wrote the United States Constitution. Yet they probably would have approved of the free and open debate over the Second Amendment that is taking place in America today.

Recently, Senator Edward Kennedy and Senator James McClure commented on the Firearm Owners Protection Bill. Senator Kennedy said that the bill damages "the fundamental effort to protect citizens from violent crime." Senator McClure commented that if the bill is passed, "People will find it a little easier to exercise their rights" to own and use guns.

Their remarks summed up the two main attitudes in America today about the right to bear arms.

Bibliography

Anderson, Jervis. *Guns in American Life*. New York: Random House, 1984.

Berger, Michael. *Firearms in American History*. New York: Watts, 1979.

Commager, Henry Steele. *The Great Constitution*. New York: Bobbs-Merrill, 1961.

Dolan, Edward F. *Gun Control*. New York: Watts, 1982.

Fincher, E. B. *The Bill of Rights*. New York: Watts, 1978.

Knight, H. V. *With Liberty and Justice for All*. Dobbs Ferry, NY: Oceana, 1967.

Montgomery, Elizabeth Rider. *Toward Democracy*. New York: Washburn, 1967.

Peterson, Helen Stone. *The Making of the United States Constitution*. Champaign, IL: Garrard, 1974.

Index